How to:
TRANSFORM
your life by
RENEWING
your mind

by

Dr. Catherine Tomlinson

How to Transform Your Life by Changing Your Mind

ABOUT THE AUTHOR

I was born into a world of contrasts, raised amidst the hustle and bustle of urban Detroit. Growing up as the middle child among three sisters and two brothers, I quickly learned the value of resilience and resourcefulness in the face of adversity.

My childhood was marked by both love and struggle. While my father worked tirelessly to provide for our family, my mother battled with addiction, leaving us to navigate the complexities of life on our own. Despite her struggles, my mother possessed a brilliant mind and a heart overflowing with love for everyone she encountered. Her presence was a beacon of light in the darkness, a reminder that even amidst our struggles, love has the power to transcend all boundaries.

As I journeyed through school, I faced the harsh realities of poverty and social stigma. Taunted and teased for not being the best dressed, I vowed to change that narrative for myself. Determined to carve out a better future, I became a hustler, balancing work and studies as a full-time college student.

It was a long and arduous journey, but in 2010, I proudly walked across the stage at Wayne State University, my mother's face beaming with pride. Two years later, she was gone, her sudden departure left a void in my heart that seemed insurmountable. Yet, even in death, my mother's spirit continued to guide me, teaching me the invaluable lesson that addiction is a disease, not a reflection of one's worth.

With a heavy heart, I threw myself into work, burying my grief beneath a mountain of responsibilities. But amidst the chaos, I found solace in caring for others, channeling my pain into purpose. It was during this time that I made the decision to pursue further education, enrolling in a Nurse Practitioner program.

As fate would have it, the COVID-19 pandemic struck during my studies, threatening to derail my dreams. But amidst uncertainty, I found clarity and purpose through spiritual awakening. Baptized in the Holy Spirit and delving into metaphysical teachings, I discovered a deeper understanding of myself and the world around me.

Through the lens of spirituality, I came to realize that true knowledge lies not in the pursuit of certainty, but in surrendering to the Divine wisdom of God and the Universe. In embracing the interconnectedness of all things, I found peace, knowing that I am guided by a higher power that transcends all understanding.

In 2021, I graduated with a Doctorate in Family Nurse Practitioner, a testament to the resilience of the Holy Spirit and the transformative power of love. As I continue my journey, I carry with me the lessons of my past, grateful for the trials that have shaped me into the person I am today—a healer, a seeker, and a vessel of divine grace.

TABLE OF CONTENTS

CHAPTER 1:

COMPONENTS OF THE SELF

All our issues as humans can be solved by first becoming aware of self. Many of us go through life longing for something higher. This longing feels like chronic discontentment that is fueled by a separation between God and us. We never seem to feel satisfied with the things we attain and the projects we do. We have forgotten Who we are and Whose we are. Well, we can begin to close this gap of separation between us and God by turning some of our attention to our internal environment instead of focusing all of our attention on external appearances.

The bible verse Genesis 15:12 says, "As the sun was setting, Abram fell into a deep sleep, and a thick and dreadful darkness came over him". Today a human can be in a "Deep Sleep", or sleep to their good, if they are unaware of their true nature. Deep sleeping can be synonymous to living in a thick and dreadful darkness, which looks like fear, anxiety, depression, anger, rage, hopelessness, boredom, and many more uncomfortable emotions, which is simply a lack of light. Therefore, if you desire to turn the lights on, then you must do what Spike Lee said in the 90's, and Wake Upppppppppppp!

Once a person wakes up to their true inner self, they will no longer be a stranger to themselves. Waking up to their good means becoming the master of their fate, the captain of their soul. The captain can choose to drive their souls from personal suffering to freedom, endless joy, inner peace, clarity of mind and the ability to live an incredibly fulfilling life. The awakened state holds everything we have ever desired and so much more. But first we must come to realize the sacred knowledge of the true inner self and all its components.

"Who looks outside dreams, who looks inside awakes"-Carl Jung

THREE INNER COMPONENTS OF THE SELF

Internally, we all have three components that make up the self. These components have been referred to as me, myself, and I. They can also be known as mind/soul, body/brain, and Holy Spirit, conscious, subconscious or super-conscious, or Ego, ID or Super-Ego. However, all the references can be used interchangeably.

<u>Me/Body/Brain/Conscious/Ego</u>

The "Me, Body/Brain, Conscious Ego", is the personality and that's the component that others meet and see. The intricate connection between Me, Body/Brain and Consciousness/Ego, forms the very essence of a person's perceived existence. Consciousness is the observed. Within the vast neural pathways of the brain consciousness arises as a symphony of electrical impulses and biochemical reactions, giving rise to thoughts, emotions, and perceptions that shapes reality.

As we navigate the complexities of our inner world, we realize that we are both the observer and the observed, intricately woven into the fabric of consciousness itself. Through self-awareness and introspection, we can explore the depths of our being, uncovering the mysteries of mind and matter. In this profound union of self and consciousness, we can find the key to unlocking the limitless potential of our human experience, transcending the boundaries of individuality to connect with the expansiveness of the universe.

<u>Myself/Mind/Soul/Subconscious/ID</u>

While the "Myself, Mind/Soul, Subconscious or ID", is the component that you mainly identify as yourself. At the heart of your existence lies a complex interplay between Myself, Mind/Soul, Subconscious, and ID. The subconscious is the essence of who you are, encompassing the totality of your being, transcending mere physical form to encompass your thoughts, emotions, and spiritual essence. Within the labyrinth of your mind, the subconscious holds control, a reservoir of memories, beliefs, and experiences that shape your perceptions and behaviors often beyond conscious awareness.

It is here that the soul, the eternal essence of your being, whispers its timeless wisdom, guiding you on the journey of self-discovery and spiritual evolution. Yet, amidst the tapestry of our inner landscape, the ego asserts its presence, the voice of self-identity and individuality, seeking validation and security in the external world. In this intricate dance between self and psyche, you strive to navigate the depths of your consciousness, seeking harmony and alignment with the higher truths of existence.

<u>I/Spirit/Super-conscious/Super-Ego</u>

Lastly, the "I, Holy Spirit, Super-Ego, or Super-Conscious", is the higher-self, spiritual-self, or the observer. At the core of our being lies a profound connection between I, Spirit, Super-Conscious, and Super-ego, which plays a unique role in shaping our experience of reality. I, the individual self, am but a vessel through which the eternal Holy Spirit flows, connecting us to the infinite wisdom and divine essence of the universe. In the realm of the super-conscious, the I am component is united with the collective consciousness of all beings, tapping into an infinite reservoir of knowledge and insight that overrides the limitations of time and space. Here, the super-ego emerges as the guiding force, the higher self that transcends egoic desires and attachments, leading you towards self-realization and spiritual fulfillment. In this sacred union of the components of self and spirit, we can find liberation from the confines of the ego, embracing the boundless potential of a person's true nature as a divine being.

These components can be compared to a person operating a gas-powered car. Where the shell of the car is our physical body; the person steering is our soul; and the gas that powers the car is the Holy Spirit. We can learn how to begin putting our cars on autopilot by allowing our inner Holy Spirit to steer the car based on the destination uploaded by our soul. The soul has been granted free choice from the Source to create its own destination.

When I was a kid, the saying used to be "Life is what you make it!". Also, I was always asked by adults, "What do you want to be when you grow up?" These questions forced me to use my imagination and believe that I could become whatever I thought I could. Well, those same principles apply today despite being an adult.

CHAPTER 2:

SELF-AWARENESS

Self-awareness is not just about knowing who we are on the surface; it's about doing the deep dive into the core of our being, understanding our true essence, and recognizing our connection to something greater than ourselves. It is the awareness of both our strengths and weaknesses, our desires and fears, and the acknowledgment of our divine inheritance. Just as Yeshua spoke of leaving behind the Holy Spirit, symbolizing the vast ocean of spiritual wisdom within each of us, so too does self-awareness unveil the infinite potential embedded within our souls.

At the center of this awakening lies the pineal gland, often referred to as the "Seat of the Soul." This small but powerful gland is believed to be the gateway to higher consciousness, where the divine meets the earthly, and the individual merges with the universal. By turning our focus inward, we unlock the treasures hidden within, tapping into a wellspring of peace, joy, love, wisdom, health, wealth, prosperity, success, and money that surpasses understanding.

To embark on the journey of self-awareness is to embark on a quest for Nirvana—a state of profound tranquility and enlightenment that transcends the turmoil and suffrage of the external world. As we turn our gaze inward, we discover that the pot of gold at the end of the rainbow lies within us, waiting to be unearthed. Here, in the depths of our being, is where the magic happens, where we find the answers to life's deepest questions and the fulfillment of our greatest desires.

Some may argue that focusing on self-awareness is selfish, but nothing could be further from the truth. In fact, it is only through knowing and loving ourselves that we can truly love and serve others. The greatest gifts of life—the peace, love, and everlasting joy we seek—are not bestowed upon us by the world but are found within the depths of our own souls. It is through self-awareness that we come to realize this truth and embrace the journey of self-love and self-discovery.

In a world plagued by chaos and division, it is time for us to be the change we wish to see. It is time to turn our attention inward, to cultivate self-awareness, and to awaken to the divine spark that resides within us all. For in the journey of self-discovery lies the key to unlocking our inner power, realizing our true potential, and creating a world filled with peace, love, and harmony.

OUR GREAT WORK

The great work that each man and woman may choose, is to know that there are not thousands of things to learn in life. There is only one thing to learn: to know the Knower within and to sincerely and regularly acknowledge God in all our ways. The kingdom of heaven is within, and we are wasting our time and defeating the work of the Holy Spirit if we look for it elsewhere. We know that the kingdom of heaven or kingdom of God is not just a place in the sky, but rather a state in the creative mind ready to be ushered in by the minds of man and woman. When we find what we were looking for, we find it was so easy. Yeshua once said, "My yoke is easy, my burden is light", meaning anything in life that's hard is not Godly, and with a solid working relationship with God, life can be so much easier. This verse, from Matthew 11:30, speaks to finding spiritual ease and comfort in following Yeshua. It suggests that living according to his teachings can bring a sense of relief and freedom from burdens. The "yoke" represents the teachings and ways of life, which are described as easy compared to the weight of worldly concerns. You work to learn that you don't have to work, the work is already done, Yeshua paid for it all. He has already saved the World. He is the truth, and the truth shall set you free from the bondage (John 8:31-32).

Many people want to be free but have yet to do their great work. We must begin to demonstrate actions that shows that we desire change. If we want happiness, health, love, success, prosperity, wealth, and money, then we must do some work. This book series will guide you on how to implement certain daily practices such as mindfulness, self-care, self-love, meditation and prayer to facilitate closing the gap between you and all your desires.

There comes a time when we realize to get different results out of life, we must try different interventions. It's like the analogy that when the dog's butt begins to hurt from sitting on a nail in the porch, he will get up. Well, it's the same with people. Once a person has suffered their fair share of heartache, depression, anxiety, worry, anger, rage, resentment, poverty, unemployment, abuse, you name it, they will begin to look for ways to change their reality. The practices in this book could be a great place to start.

We often try to change the things, people, and situations in our external environment, without ever doing the work on the inside environment. We fail to realize that everything in our life is happening for us, not to us. We each are responsible for our own experiences. Every thought we think is shaping our future. The situations that occur today, began with yesterday's thoughts, or last week's thoughts, or last year thoughts. With our thoughts we create every so-called illness in our body. If these concepts bring any doubt in your mind, at least try them. You will never know if they work if you never try to work them. Exactly, what do you stand to lose?

"Death and life are in the power of the tongue"-Proverbs 18:21

CHAPTER 3:

HOW TO TUNE INTO THE INNER-SELF

By tuning into your inner-self one can connect deeply with their true thoughts, feelings, and desires beyond external distractions and expectations. It involves becoming more aware of your emotions, noticing patterns in your thinking, and listening to your inner knowing. This type of introspection requires a slowing down and quieting of the mind. By cultivating a quiet mind to observe the inner chatter and environment, one can better understand their values and motivations. This understanding can assist with making decisions that align with one's authentic self. Tuning into the inner self, is a practice that can foster greater self-compassion, resilience, and clarity in navigating life's challenges.

DEEP BREATHING

Deep breathing serves as a bridge between the mind, body, and soul. By taking slow deep breaths, one can calm their nervous system, making it easier to enter a mindful or meditative state where we connect with our inner essence. Many spiritual traditions view breath as a life force or energy (prana or chi), which nourishes and revitalizes the spirit. Through deep breathing, we can raise our awareness, energy and mood. Deep breathing also sends oxygenated blood to your organs which can promote overall healing in the body. If we stop breathing for more than three minutes, we will lose consciousness. However, our hearts and brains would continue to function. Therefore, not only is breathing sustaining oxygenation, but it also sustains consciousness. So, when we deep breath, we are taking in larger doses of God.

MINDFULNESS

By understanding and implementing daily practices such as mindfulness a person can begin to slow their daily life down long enough to cultivate peace and solitude in their inner world. Mindfulness requires a deliberate effort to stop all thoughts constantly circulating in the brain. It is the art of noticing and quieting your thoughts, while using all your sense organs to remain aware of what is happening in the current moment. Mindfulness requires a person to bring their Spirit/Observer self to the fore front. The observer or spiritual self can see and experience different situations, it observes, assimilates words/thoughts and prepares desires, without judgment.

Mindfulness is a form of meditation training a person on how to control their thoughts, and how to avoid allowing one's thoughts to control them. Thoughts are like wild monkeys in our head, and they seem hard to control. If they are allowed the ruminate into past events, they can lead to feelings of depression. In contrast, if thoughts are allowed to ruminate into the predicted future, they lead to feelings of anxiety. Therefore, changing and redirecting your thoughts and intentions to stay in the current moment is what this mind science is all about. "Do not conform to the patterns of this world but be transformed by the renewing of your mind" (Romans 12:2).

One can practice mindfulness while walking down the street, eating a delicious meal, cleaning, spending time in nature, sitting by or in a body of water, taking a bath, burning essential oils or incense, reading a book or by walking with your bare feet in the grass or soil, a practice known as Grounding.

GROUNDING

Grounding is the process of reconnecting with the Earth/Gaia to promote healing and recharging. We can all be compared to a battery that contains stored energy with either a positive or negative current, that requires recharging just like our cellphones. The benefit of grounding includes enhanced emotional and mental clarity, reduction of blood pressure, stress and anxiety, and a general sense of well-being. When practiced consistently it will keep your emotional and thought system balanced, it will also revitalize your energies.

MEDITATION

Meditation is like taking a vacation for your mind—it's a special time when you can relax, recharge, and find inner peace. Imagine sitting quietly in a comfortable place, closing your eyes, and taking slow, deep breaths. As you breathe in and out, you let go of any worries or stress and focus only on the present moment. Meditation is a way to quiet your inner chit chat, to hear your spiritual guidance system whispering words of wisdom. That's what meditation is all about—it's a simple practice that can have powerful effects on your mental, emotional, and even physical well-being.

When you meditate, it's like giving your brain a chance to rest and reset. Studies have shown that meditation can help reduce stress, improve concentration, and increase feelings of calm and happiness. It's like pressing a pause button on the hustle and bustle of everyday life and giving yourself the gift of stillness and silence. Whether you're feeling anxious, overwhelmed, or just need a break from the chaos of the world, meditation is a powerful tool that can help you find peace and clarity amidst the noise.

PRAYING

Prayer can be considered talking to your inner spiritual guidance system. In true prayer we use our words to talk to God and turn our attention inwards to involve some meditation on those words. Then we wait in stillness and silence for God to answer those prayers. Therefore, even to effectively pray, you must include a portion of meditation. Prayer can be said to be "taking hold of God's willingness". Simply, God wants for us what we want for ourselves. Your job is to check in with self, to see exactly what you are telling God that you want? We all have free choice, because God is gracious like that. Even Christ Yeshua forbid all prayers of doubt, but said, "All things that you pray and ask for, believe that you have already received them, and you shall have them" (Mark 11:24).

AFFIRMATIONS

Affirmations are like magic words that we use to create positive changes in our lives. They're short, simple phrases that we speak to ourselves repeatedly, like a mantra or a prayer. Affirmations help us focus on what we want to manifest in our lives, whether it's confidence, success, or happiness. By repeating affirmations regularly, we can train our minds to think more positively and attract more of what we desire into our lives.

Imagine affirmations as seeds that we plant in the garden of our minds. When we repeat them consistently, we water and nourish these seeds, helping them grow into strong and healthy beliefs. Affirmations can be tailored to our specific goals and desires, whether it's improving our self-esteem, overcoming challenges, or achieving our dreams. They're like little reminders that we carry with us throughout the day, helping us stay focused and motivated on our journey towards greater happiness and fulfillment.

CHAPTER 4:
THE POWER OF WORDS AND THOUGHTS

WORDS

Words are magnetic. Positive words carry a positive charge, and negative words carry a negative charge. We are electrical beings, not just chemical beings. We have a system of electricity powering our bodies, known as the nervous system. The nervous system consists of the brain and the spinal cord. When thoughts are received from the immaterial universe, they are converted by the brain through electrical currents in the neuron synaptic gap. It's all energy just like the stuff we see in the electrical socket when it misfires, or when a person is electrocuted. This same type of electrical charge is applied to our words when we release them; giving them the power to attract a like charge.

In the beginning was the word, and the word was God, and the word is God (Genesis 1:2).

THOUGHTS

Your thoughts consist of a compilation of your words. Thoughts create things. We are what we think. Therefore, if we change what we think, then we can change what we are. We are all sons and daughter of The Most High, The King, The Creator, The Source, God, Christ, Allah, whatever you refer to "It" as, we all come from the same place. It's time we start knowing and acting like we know Who we are and Whose we are. We are Divine Beings, who come from the One Supreme Being. Once we learn who we are and that we are made in the exact same image of God, just the way we are made from the genetic image of our Earth mothers and fathers, we will be able to do the same things that Yeshua did. "He that believe in me, the works that I do, so shall he also do, and even greater works shall he do" (John 14:12-18). Yeshua wasn't talking about our ego selves, but our spiritual selves can do these greater works.

According to the bible, "As a man thinketh, so he is" (Proverbs 23:7). Therefore, you get exactly what you constantly think about. In quantum physics there is a great explanation behind this concept, also known as the "Law of Attraction". When magnetic emotions are released, they radiate out into the environment like radio-waves or microwaves, carrying the attached thought. Based on the frequency and sustainability of the thought, its matched with an emotion of the same frequency. Everyone has a auric field which is an invisible colorful ring around them that can potentially expand in each direction up to 9 ft based on their sustained thought, emotion and frequency.

If a negative low vibrational frequency thought is sustained for 17 seconds or greater, that causes emotions such as fear, shame, guilt, rage, or anger, then it will shrink off your auric field. In comparison, if it's a positive high vibrational frequency thought that is sustained for 17 seconds or greater that causes emotions such as love, joy, peace, enlightenment, or happiness, then the auric field will expand. A widened auric field has a stronger electromagnetic pull which can produce an attraction to physical matter. A contracted field carries a weak electromagnetic pull will have no effect on matter.

For any of these concepts to have meaning, we must suspend our current belief system. With a belief in your true spiritual soul-self, comes an element of surrender to the Divine magic of the spiritual world. This Divine magic has the power to forever change the game of life as we know it. What we think and feel on the inside determines what we experience on the outside. Our thoughts and words both carry a magnetic charge, which can attract its kind.

LAW OF ATTRACTION

Everything that's coming into your life you are attracting into your life. And it's attracted to you by virtue of the images you're holding in your mind. It's what you're thinking. It's what you are saying with your inner voice and your outer voice. Whatever is going on in your inner mind, you are attracting it in your outer life. If you have expensive thoughts like love, happiness, health, success, prosperity, money and wealth, then you attract just that. On the other hand, if you have cheap thoughts such as poverty, ill health, loneliness, emptiness, hopelessness, it also gives you these things because that's what you're projecting out from your inner thoughts.

METAPHYSICS

Metaphysics is like exploring the mysteries of the universe—it's a branch of philosophy that asks big questions about the nature of reality, existence, and consciousness. Imagine it as a treasure map leading to hidden treasures of wisdom and understanding. Metaphysics seeks to understand the fundamental nature of reality beyond what we can see, touch, or measure. It delves into concepts like time, space, causality, and consciousness, exploring how they shape our perceptions of the world around us.

One way to think about metaphysics is as a journey of discovery, where we explore the deeper truths that lie beneath the surface of everyday life. It's like peeling back the layers of an onion to reveal the core of existence. Metaphysics invites us to ponder the big questions of life, such as: What is the meaning of existence? What is the nature of consciousness? And what is the relationship between the mind and the body? By delving into these questions with an open mind and a curious spirit, we can gain new insights into the nature of reality and our place within it.

Therefore, if a person mindfully works on managing their thoughts, feelings, and desires with these practices you can attract it all. Guess this explains how the rich only gets richer, because they have implemented this practice and proven to themselves that it works, so why stop using it? No wonder it's also known as "The Secret" and hence has been kept a secret from the impoverished.

A woman once asked a rich man, "What's your secret to being rich?" But no-one ever asks a poor man his secret to being poor! If you desire prosperity, then you must follow those that are prosperous instead of those who are in survival mode. For "We shall delight in the Law of the Lord and in his law do we meditate day and night, and we shall be like a tree planted by the rivers of water that bring forth fruit and his leaf shall not wither, and whatsoever he does shall prosper" (Psalm 1). This secret gives you anything that you think and want, without fail. The Source/ God wants each one of us to be prosperous, it's our divine right and inheritance as sons and daughters of the King. However, it is also your right to experience poverty and suffering.

-The choice is yours, "You can get with this, or you can get that! -Tribe Called Quest

CHAPTER 5:

HOW TO PRACTICE SELF CARE

SELF-CARE

Self-care is a fundamental aspect of nurturing our well-being and sustaining prosperity in our lives. In this extended discussion, we'll delve deeper into some key components of self-care and how they contribute to our overall prosperity. The practice of self-care can assist with tuning into your inner thoughts and feelings. Self-care means taking time to practice solitude and mindfully focus on things like love, gratitude, faith, emotions, appearance, joy, peace, forgiveness and happiness to promote physical, emotional, and spiritual health. We must begin to turn off our intellect and go inside to be with self. It can also help to better manage energy and confidence levels, everyday stressors, and financial concerns.

Self-care cultivates self-love, which in turn increases self-awareness. These practices require an effortless effort that is well worth the by-product. The only way these practices can work for an individual is if they work with them. Faith without action is dead. We must understand that developing self-care, self-love, and self-awareness is an inside job, that can only be done by you. The simple practices such as love, gratitude, faith, emotional intelligence, appearance, joy, peace, boundaries, forgiveness, faith, healthy eating, cleanliness, good sleep, movement, intimacy, music, chakra balancing and managing energy stores, can be implemented to guide us to self-care, self-love, and self-awareness. Once these practices have been cultivated, everything in life begins to make more sense.

LOVE

Love can heal all things. God is Love. We are love. Love is the thing that helps us to thrive instead of just surviving. Love is the fundamental force that underlies all of creation. Love is a potent healing force that has the power to turn pain into wholeness and darkness into light. In the field of energy medicine, love is recognized as the ultimate remedy for restoring balance and harmony to the body, mind, and soul. Through practices such as heart-centered meditation, Reiki, and vibrational healing, we harness the transformative power of love to dissolve energetic blockages, release old stale patterns, and cultivate radiant well-being. We come to realize that love is not just a fleeting emotion or romantic ideal but the very essence of our existence—the Alpha and Omega, the beginning and end of all that is. In the embrace of love, we find solace, meaning, and purpose, and in its radiant glow, we discover the truth of who we are—eternal beings of love, forever entwined in the dance of creation.

GRATITUDE

Gratitude attracts abundance and prosperity. Always be grateful. Practicing gratitude is a powerful form of self-care that can profoundly impact our mindset and outlook on life. When we cultivate a sense of gratitude, we shift our focus from what we lack to what we have, fostering feelings of abundance and contentment. Research has shown that regularly expressing gratitude can improve mental health, reduce stress, and enhance overall well-being.

One way to incorporate gratitude into our daily lives is by keeping a gratitude journal, where we write down three things we're thankful for each day. This simple practice can help us develop a more positive perspective and cultivate an attitude of appreciation for the blessings in our lives, both big and small.

FAITH

"According to your faith, so be it onto you" (Matt 9:29). Faith is the substance for all things hoped for. It's the expectancy for things not seen. Faith gives you the ability to rest in knowing that your desire will be delivered right to your doorstep after placing your order, the same way we order a package from Amazon, and expect the item on the delivery date. When we desire anything in life, we must be precise in our asking and feel as if we already have that thing. After ordering our package we must surrender in knowing that God is going to deliver just like the UPS driver, but not on our time because He doesn't wear a watch, but on His time. When we ask for something by giving thanks for it has already been supplied, the desire comes to us faster. Faith holds your vision steady, and the adverse pictures are dissolved and dissipated. In due season we will all reap what we sow. When you plant a seed in the garden you understand the fruit is in the seed, and it takes time to grow. If you stand around and stare at the seed you can't capture it growing in front of your eyes, so you stop watching and the plant sprouts. We must keep this same energy when we pray and desire things.

EMOTIONS

Emotions are like signals that our bodies send to our brains, telling us how we feel about something. They come from our thoughts and words, and they can be powerful. Imagine them like little messengers, telling us important things about ourselves and the world around us. Sometimes, they make us feel happy, excited, or calm, but other times, they might make us feel sad, angry, or scared. It's important to pay attention to our emotions because they can help guide us through life. By tuning in when we feel them and asking ourselves why we feel that way, we can learn a lot about ourselves and the situations we're in. It's like having a compass that helps us navigate our feelings and make choices that are best for us. Once we understand our emotions better, we can use them to help us, rather than letting them control us. Emotional intelligence is like a superpower that helps us make sense of our feelings and use them wisely. So, next time you feel an emotion, take a moment to listen to what it's trying to tell you—it might just lead you in the right direction.

APPEARANCE

Taking care of how we look on the outside is important because it can show how we feel on the inside. When we take care of ourselves and look neat and tidy, it can help us feel good about ourselves and boost our confidence. It's like sending a message to others that we care about ourselves and take pride in how we present ourselves to the world. On the other hand, if we don't take care of our appearance, it might make us feel less confident and affect how others see us.

Sometimes, our outer appearance can even reflect what's going on inside our minds and hearts. When we're feeling happy, peaceful, or confident on the inside, it can show through in how we look on the outside. It's like our appearance can reflect our inner thoughts and feelings. And when we're spiritually connected or in tune with ourselves, it's like our outer appearance takes on a life of its own, radiating positivity and inner peace. So, taking care of how we look isn't just about how others see us—it's also about how we feel about ourselves and the energy we project into the world.

Not to mention that when someone has a close relationship with God, they can maintain a youthful outer look. Firstly, when someone has a strong spiritual connection, they often experience a sense of inner peace, joy, and contentment. This inner state of well-being can radiate outward, contributing to a more youthful and vibrant appearance. Additionally, spiritual practices such as prayer, meditation, and gratitude can reduce stress levels, which can in turn slow down the aging process and promote overall health and vitality.

Furthermore, a close relationship with God often involves practicing self-care and treating the body as a temple. This can include eating nourishing foods, exercising regularly, getting enough rest, and avoiding harmful substances. By taking care of the physical body, individuals can maintain a more youthful appearance and prolong their overall health and vitality.

Moreover, a deep connection with God can provide a sense of purpose and meaning in life, which can inspire individuals to live with passion and enthusiasm. This zest for life can manifest in a youthful energy and vitality that is evident in both appearance and demeanor.

JOY

Joy is like a special kind of happiness that fills our hearts with warmth and light. It's more than just feeling happy for a moment—it's a deep sense of delight and contentment that lasts a long time. Joy can come from many different things, like spending time with loved ones, doing things we love, or even just appreciating the beauty of nature around us. When we feel joyful, it's like our hearts are singing with happiness, and everything feels brighter and more wonderful.

Having joy in our lives is important because it helps us feel good about ourselves and the world around us. When we're joyful, it's like we're shining a light that spreads happiness to everyone we meet. It can make us more hopeful, kinder, and more grateful for the things we have. Joy can also help us feel more resilient and stronger when things get tough, like a little spark of light in the darkness. So, it's important to find things that bring us joy and hold onto them tightly, because joy is like a special treasure that makes life more beautiful and meaningful.

PEACE

Peace is like a calm, quiet river flowing gently through our hearts and minds. It's a feeling of tranquility and harmony that helps us feel safe and happy. When we have peace in our lives, it's like all the worries and stresses melt away, and we can just relax and enjoy the moment. Peace can come from many different places, like spending time in nature, practicing mindfulness, or being with people we love. It's like a warm blanket that wraps around us, making us feel cozy and content.

Having peace in our lives is important because it helps us feel balanced and centered. When we're at peace, we're better able to handle the ups and downs of life with grace and resilience. It can help us make better decisions and be kinder to ourselves and others. Peace also helps us feel more connected to the world around us, like we're part of something bigger and more beautiful. So, it's imperative to find moments of peace in our busy lives and hold onto them tightly, because peace is like a precious gift that brings joy and serenity to our hearts.

BOUNDARIES

Boundaries are like invisible lines that help us understand where we end and where others begin. They're like fences around our feelings, thoughts, and personal space, helping us feel safe and respected. When we have healthy boundaries, it's like we're protecting ourselves from things that might hurt us or make us uncomfortable. Boundaries can come in many forms, like saying "no" when we don't want to do something or telling someone when they've crossed a line. It's like setting rules for how we want to be treated and making sure those rules are respected.

Having boundaries is important because it helps us feel in control of our lives and relationships. When we know our limits and communicate them clearly, it helps prevent misunderstandings and conflicts with others. Boundaries also help us prioritize our own needs and well-being, instead of always putting others first. They're like a shield that protects us from getting overwhelmed or taken advantage of. So, it's important to learn about boundaries and practice setting them in our daily lives, because they help us feel empowered and respected.

FORGIVENESS

Forgiveness is like a special gift we give to ourselves and others. It's when we choose to let go of anger and hurt feelings, and instead, choose to show kindness and understanding. In the Bible, there are many stories about forgiveness, like when Jesus forgave those who hurt him, even when it was hard. One of the most famous verses about forgiveness is from Matthew 6:14-15, where it says, "For if you forgive other people when they sin against you, your heavenly Father will also forgive you. But if you do not forgive others their sins, your Father will not forgive your sins." This means that when we forgive others, we also receive forgiveness from God.

Forgiveness is important because it helps us heal and move forward from painful experiences. When we hold onto grudges and anger, it's like drinking poison with the hopes of killing someone else. But when we forgive, it's like lifting that burden off our shoulders and feeling free again. Forgiveness also helps restore peace and harmony in our relationships, because it allows us to let go of resentment and build trust and understanding. So, it's important to remember the power of forgiveness and practice it in our lives, because it brings healing and peace to our hearts and the world around us.

HEALTHY EATING

Fueling our bodies with nutritious foods is another essential aspect of self-care. Consuming high-energy foods such as fruits and vegetables provide our bodies with the vital nutrients they need to function optimally. These foods are packed with vitamins, minerals, and antioxidants that support cellular health, boost immunity, and promote overall vitality. It's crucial to prioritize whole, unprocessed foods and minimize the consumption of processed foods, which can be detrimental to our health. As the saying goes, "You are what you eat," and nourishing our bodies with wholesome foods is key to maintaining physical and mental well-being.

Bodies are constantly regenerating cells, which typically have a life span of seven years, depending on the type of cell. The bodies that we once had as infants, children and young adults, are not the same bodies that we have as older adults and seniors. These processes of regeneration require the proper building blocks like a Lego set. If one piece is missing, havoc can be reached. The body is intricate and complex, and it requires the proper nutrients. Therefore, eating healthy whole foods, without the consumption of processed food, which is considered any food in a bag or box, is imperative to the body's structure and function. Junk in junk out. We are what we consume. This includes the food and the word of God. "Man shall not live on bread alone, but on every word that proceeds out of the mouth of God"-Matthew 4:4. Many people place a lot of emphasis on consuming food. Just like many categories in our lives, diversity is key.

CLEANLINESS

Maintaining a clean and organized environment is an integral part of self-care that can have a significant impact on our mental clarity and emotional well-being. When our surroundings are clutter-free and tidy, it's easier to focus, think clearly, and feel calm and grounded.

Taking time to declutter and organize our living space can be a form of self-care. It allows us to create a peaceful and harmonious environment that supports our overall health and happiness. Even simple tasks like making the bed in the morning can have a profound effect on our mood and productivity throughout the day. A noticeable decline in the cleanliness of a person's body and environment are early signs of a depressed mood. Therefore, it's logical to believe that upon bathing and cleaning up your space can improve your mental and spiritual health. When a person emerges their body in water, it washes away negative charged atoms, known as ions. This practice alone can make a person feel so rejuvenated and enlivened afterwards.

GOOD SLEEP PATERNS

Getting an adequate amount of quality sleep is essential for our physical and mental health. Sleep plays a crucial role in repairing and rejuvenating the body, consolidating memories, and regulating mood and emotions. Poor sleep quality or insufficient sleep can lead to a host of health issues, including fatigue, sustained inflammation, irritability, inability to lose weight, and impaired cognitive function.

Developing good sleep hygiene practices can help promote restful sleep and improve overall sleep quality. This includes establishing a consistent sleep schedule, creating a relaxing bedtime routine, and creating a comfortable sleep environment free of distractions.

MOVEMENTS

Regular physical activity is essential for maintaining physical health, reducing stress, and promoting overall well-being. Exercise releases endorphins, which are neurotransmitters that help alleviate stress and boost mood. It also improves cardiovascular health, strengthens muscles and bones, and enhances flexibility and balance. Finding activities that you enjoy and incorporating them into your daily routine can make exercise feel more like self-care than a chore. Whether it's going for a walk in nature, practicing yoga, or participating in a group fitness class, finding ways to move your body regularly can have a profound impact on your physical and mental health.

INTIMACY

Nurturing intimate connections with others is an important aspect of self-care that contributes to our emotional well-being and sense of belonging. Whether it's romantic relationships, friendships, or familial bonds, meaningful connections with others provide us with support, love, and a sense of connection. By taking time to prioritize and cultivate these relationships is essen-

tial for fostering intimacy and building strong, fulfilling connections. This can involve spending quality time together, engaging
in open and honest communication, and expressing appreciation
and affection for one another.

MUSIC

Music and sound have a remarkable ability to touch our souls
and lift our spirits. Imagine the feeling of listening to your fa-
vorite song and feeling a wave of calm wash over you, or the joy
that fills your heart when you hear birds chirping on a sunny
morning. These experiences are not just coincidences—they are
examples of the powerful ways in which music and sound can
spiritually heal us. Whether it's the soothing melody of a piano,
the rhythmic beat of a drum, or the harmonious sound of a choir,
music has the power to connect us to something greater than
ourselves and uplift our spirits in times of need.

Sound therapy, also known as sound healing, is a practice
that has been used for centuries to promote physical, emotional, and spiritual well-being. By using specific tones, frequencies,
and vibrations, sound therapists believe they can help balance
the body's energy centers, or chakras, and promote healing on
a deeper level. Whether it's using singing bowls, tuning forks, or
chanting, sound therapy can help release tension, reduce stress,
and promote a sense of peace and relaxation. For many people,
the healing power of music and sound is not just a belief—it's a
profound and transformative experience that can bring comfort,
solace, and healing to the mind, body, and soul.

CHAKRAS

Chakras are like energy centers in our bodies that help keep
us balanced and healthy. Imagine them as spinning wheels of
light that run from the base of your spine to the top of your head.
Each chakra is associated with a different color and has its own
unique purpose. For example, the root chakra, located at the base

40

of the spine, helps us feel grounded and safe, while the heart chakra, located in the center of the chest, helps us feel love and compassion. By keeping our chakras in balance, we can feel more energized, focused, and at peace.

To maintain the energy of our chakras, it's important to take care of ourselves both physically and emotionally. One way to do this is through practices like yoga, meditation, and deep breathing exercises, which can help open and align our chakras. Eating a healthy diet, getting enough sleep, and staying active can also help keep our chakras balanced and energized. Additionally, spending time in nature, surrounding ourselves with positive people, and practicing self-care can help us maintain the energy of our chakras and feel more vibrant and alive. By paying attention to our bodies and taking steps to nourish our chakras, we can create a greater sense of harmony and well-being in our lives.

ENERGY

Energy is like the fuel that powers our bodies and minds—it's what keeps us feeling alive, alert, and ready to take on the day. Just like a battery needs to be charged to work properly, our bodies need to be filled with energy to function at their best. One way to maintain our energy is by taking care of ourselves physically. This means eating a healthy diet full of fruits, vegetables, and whole grains, getting enough sleep each night, and staying active through exercise and play. When we take care of our bodies, we give them the energy they need to keep us feeling strong and energized.

Another way to maintain our energy is by taking care of ourselves emotionally and mentally. This means taking time to relax and unwind, whether it's through meditation, deep breathing exercises, or spending time with friends and family. It also means doing things that make us happy and bring us joy, like pursuing hobbies we love or spending time in nature. When we take care of our emotional and mental well-being, we give ourselves the energy we need to stay positive, focused, and resilient in the face of life's challenges. By balancing our physical, emotional, and mental health, we can maintain our energy and live our lives to the fullest.

In conclusion, self-care is an essential practice for nurturing our physical, emotional, and spiritual well-being. By incorporating practices such as gratitude, healthy eating, cleanliness, good sleep patterns, movement, and intimacy into our daily lives, we can cultivate a greater sense of prosperity and fulfillment. Remember, investing in yourself is not selfish; it's necessary for living a happy, healthy, and prosperous life.

CHAPTER 6:
THE POWER OF SELF-LOVE

Self-love is the best love. When one truly loves self, they can finally love others. It is a profound and transformative concept that lies at the core of our well-being and personal growth. It encompasses acceptance, compassion, and appreciation for oneself, regardless of imperfections or shortcomings. The true love that one search for in others, first must be found in themselves. True self-love can display itself as being content spending time alone in solitude, developing boundaries and preferences, speaking up for yourself and your inner child, ceasing from people pleasing and commencing to God-pleasing, placing distance between yourself and others who no longer serve your highest good, living as an adult, but playing like a kid, and developing hobbies.

In this discussion, we will explore the importance of self-love, its impact on various aspects of our lives, and practical strategies for cultivating a greater sense of love and acceptance for ourselves.

UNDERSTANDING SELF-LOVE

At its essence, self-love is about recognizing and valuing our inherent worth as individuals. It involves treating ourselves with kindness, respect, and compassion, just as we would treat a dear friend or loved one. Self-love means embracing all aspects of ourselves - the light and the shadow, the strengths and the weaknesses - without judgment or self-criticism.

Contrary to popular belief, self-love is not about ego or narcissism. It's about developing a healthy and balanced relationship with self, one that fosters confidence, resilience, and emotional well-being. When we practice self-love, we acknowledge our own needs, prioritize self-care, and set boundaries that honor our values and worth.

THE IMPORTANCE OF SELF-LOVE

Self-love is fundamental to our overall health and happiness. When we love and accept ourselves unconditionally, we cultivate a sense of inner peace and fulfillment that radiates outward into every aspect of our lives. Here are some ways in which self-love impacts various areas of our well-being:

1. **Emotional Well-Being:** Self-love fosters emotional resilience and helps us navigate life's challenges with greater ease and grace. When we love ourselves unconditionally, we're less likely to be swayed by external validation or criticism, and we're better equipped to handle setbacks and disappointments.

2. **Relationships:** Cultivating self-love is essential for building healthy and fulfilling relationships with others. When we love and accept ourselves, we're able to show up authentically in our interactions with others, setting the foundation for genuine connections based on mutual respect and understanding.

3. **Physical Health:** Research has shown that self-love is associated with better physical health outcomes, including lower levels of stress, improved immune function, and reduced risk of chronic diseases. When we prioritize self-care and listen to our bodies' needs, we're better able to maintain optimal health and vitality.

4. **Personal Growth:** Self-love is a catalyst for personal growth and transformation. When we believe in ourselves and our abilities, we're more willing to take risks, pursue our passions, and step outside of our comfort zones. Self-love empowers us to embrace our full potential and live life to the fullest.

CULTIVATING SELF-LOVE

While self-love is inherent to our being, it's also a skill that can be cultivated and nurtured over time. Here are some practical strategies for cultivating a greater sense of self-love in your life:

1. **Practice Self-Compassion:** Treat yourself with the same kindness and understanding that you would offer to a friend facing a difficult situation. Practice self-compassion by acknowledging your struggles and imperfections without judgment and offering yourself words of encouragement and support.

2. **Set Healthy Boundaries:** Learn to say no to things that don't align with your values or priorities and prioritize your own needs and well-being. Setting healthy boundaries is essential for protecting your energy and preserving your sense of self-worth.

3. **Practice Gratitude:** Cultivate an attitude of gratitude by regularly reflecting on the things you appreciate about yourself and your life. Keep a gratitude journal where you write down three things you're thankful for each day and take time to savor the positive moments and experiences in your life.

4. **Engage in Self-Care:** Prioritize self-care activities that nourish your mind, body, and soul. This can include things like getting enough sleep, eating nutritious foods, beauty care, exercising regularly, spending time in nature, and engaging in activities that bring you joy and fulfillment.

5. **Challenge Negative Self-Talk:** Pay attention to the way you speak to yourself and challenge negative self-talk when it arises. Replace self-critical thoughts with more compassionate and empowering affirmations that affirm your worth and potential.

In conclusion, self-love is a powerful force that has the potential to transform our lives from the inside out. By cultivating a greater sense of love, acceptance, and compassion for ourselves, we can unlock our true potential and live a life filled with joy, purpose, and fulfillment. Remember, you are worthy of love and deserving of all the blessings life has to offer. Embrace yourself fully and watch as the magic of self-love unfolds in your life.

CHAPTER 7:
THE POWER OF SELF-AWARENESS

Self-awareness is a foundational skill that forms the basis of personal development and fulfillment. It involves introspection, reflection, and an honest understanding of oneself – including strengths, weaknesses, values, beliefs, emotions, and motivations. In this discussion, we will explore the importance of self-awareness, its benefits, and practical strategies for cultivating greater self-awareness in our lives.

UNDERSTANDING SELF-AWARENESS

Self-awareness is the ability to observe and understand our thoughts, feelings, and behaviors without judgment. It involves being attuned to our inner experiences and recognizing how they influence our actions and interactions with the world around us. Self-awareness is a journey of self-discovery that requires courage, curiosity, and a willingness to explore the depths of our inner landscape.

There are two primary components of self-awareness:

1. **Internal Self-Awareness:** This involves understanding our own thoughts, feelings, values, and beliefs. Internal self-awareness allows us to recognize our emotions as they arise, understand the underlying reasons for our behaviors, and identify patterns and themes in our thoughts and feelings.

2. **External Self-Awareness:** This involves understanding how we are perceived by others and how our actions impact those around us. External self-awareness allows us to see ourselves through the eyes of others, recognize how

our behavior affects our relationships, and adapt our actions accordingly.

THE IMPORTANCE OF SELF AWARENESS

Self-awareness is essential for personal growth, emotional intelligence, and meaningful relationships. Here are some reasons why self-awareness is so important:

1. **Personal Growth:** Self-awareness is the cornerstone of personal growth and development. By understanding ourselves more deeply, we can identify areas for improvement, set meaningful goals, and take intentional steps toward becoming the best version of ourselves.

2. **Emotional Intelligence:** Self-awareness is a key component of emotional intelligence, which is the ability to recognize, understand, and manage our own emotions as well as the emotions of others. By developing self-awareness, we can regulate our emotions more effectively, empathize with others, and navigate interpersonal relationships with greater skill and sensitivity.

3. **Authenticity and Integrity:** Self-awareness enables us to live authentically and align our actions with our values and beliefs. When we have a clear understanding of who we are and what matters most to us, we can make choices that are congruent with our true selves, leading to greater integrity and fulfillment.

4. **Effective Communication:** Self-awareness enhances our ability to communicate effectively with others. By understanding our own communication style, preferences, and biases, we can express ourselves more clearly, listen more attentively, and navigate conflicts and misunderstandings with greater empathy and understanding.

CULTIVATING SELF-AWARENESS

While self-awareness is a natural capacity of the human mind, it's also a skill that can be developed and strengthened over time. Here are some practical strategies for cultivating greater self-awareness in your life:

1. **Practice Mindfulness:** Mindfulness involves paying attention to the present moment with openness, curiosity, and acceptance. By practicing mindfulness meditation, mindful breathing, or other mindfulness techniques, you can develop greater awareness of your thoughts, feelings, and sensations as they arise.

2. **Journaling:** Keeping a journal can be a powerful tool for self-reflection and self-discovery. Take time each day to write about your thoughts, feelings, and experiences, and explore any patterns or insights that emerge. Writing can help clarify your thoughts, process emotions, and gain perspective on your life.

3. **Seek Feedback:** Solicit feedback from trusted friends, family members, or colleagues about your strengths, weaknesses, and blind spots. Be open to constructive criticism and use it as an opportunity for growth and self-improvement.

4. **Reflect on Past Experiences:** Take time to reflect on past experiences, both positive and negative, and consider how they have shaped your beliefs, values, and behaviors. Reflective practices such as journaling, meditation, or therapy can help you gain insight into your motivations, fears, and aspirations.

5. **Practice Self-Compassion:** Cultivate a compassionate attitude toward yourself, especially during times of difficulty or struggle. Treat yourself with kindness, understanding, and patience, and remember that self-awareness is a journey, not a destination. Embrace your imperfections and celebrate your progress along the way.

In conclusion, self-awareness is a foundational skill that empowers us to live more authentically, compassionately, and intentionally. By cultivating greater self-awareness, we can unlock our full potential, nurture meaningful relationships, and live a life of purpose and fulfillment. Remember, the journey of self-awareness is ongoing, and each moment offers an opportunity for growth and self-discovery. Embrace the journey with curiosity, openness, and a willingness to explore the depths of your own being.

CHAPTER 8:

INNER CHILD TRAUMA & HEALING

Inner child trauma is like a hidden hurt that we carry inside us from when we were young. It's when something bad or scary happened to us when we were kids, and it still affects us now, even though we might not realize it. This kind of trauma can come from many different things, like being bullied, losing a loved one, or not feeling loved or safe at home. Even though we grow up and become adults, that hurt from our past can still stay with us and affect how we feel and act today.

Inner child trauma can happen in many ways, and it's different for everyone. Sometimes, it's a big event that happens all at once, like a car accident or a natural disaster. Other times, it's something that happens repeatedly, like being yelled at or ignored by the people who are supposed to take care of us. These experiences can make us feel scared, sad, or even angry. They can also make us feel like we're not good enough or that we don't deserve to be loved.

Understanding our inner child trauma is important because it helps us heal and feel better about ourselves. Sometimes, we might not even realize that we're still carrying around that hurt from our past. But when we take the time to look inside ourselves and understand where those feelings are coming from, it's like shining a light on the dark corners of our hearts and minds. It helps us make sense of our feelings and behaviors, and it gives us the power to change and grow.

When we have inner child trauma, it can affect us in many ways. For example, it can make us feel anxious or depressed, like we're always on edge or that we can't trust anyone. It can also affect the way we see ourselves and the world around us. We might feel like we're not good enough or that we don't deserve to be happy. Inner child trauma can also affect the way we behave, like making us act out or push people away when we're feeling scared or hurt. So, it's important to be kind to ourselves and give us the love and care that our inner child needs to heal and thrive.

HEALING CHILD TRAUMA

When we experience inner child trauma, it's like carrying around a heavy backpack filled with hurt and pain from our past. But just like we can lighten our load by taking out some of the things in our backpack, we can also heal our inner child trauma by learning new ways to cope and heal. Healing from inner child trauma is like going on a journey of self-discovery, where we learn to understand our feelings, take care of ourselves, and find new ways to feel happy and safe.

The first step in healing from inner child trauma is to understand our feelings and where they come from. This means taking the time to think about the things that happened to us when we were young and how they make us feel now. It's okay to feel sad, angry, or scared about what happened, but it's also important to remember that those feelings don't have to control us. By talking about our feelings with someone we trust, like a therapist, parent, teacher, or counselor, we can start to make sense of them and learn new ways to cope.

Taking care of ourselves is another important part of healing from inner child trauma. This means doing things that make us feel happy and safe, like spending time with friends and family, doing hobbies we enjoy, or spending time in nature. It also means taking care of our bodies by eating healthy foods, getting enough sleep, and exercising regularly. When we take care of ourselves, it's like giving our inner child the love and care they need to heal and grow.

Finding new ways to cope with our feelings is another important part of healing from inner child trauma. This might mean learning new skills, like deep breathing or meditation, to help us feel calm when we're feeling anxious or stressed. It might also mean setting boundaries with people who make us feel uncomfortable or unsafe, or finding ways to express our feelings through art, music, or writing. No matter what, it's important to remember that healing from inner child trauma takes time and effort, but with patience and perseverance, we can learn to heal and grow from our past experiences.

CHAPTER 9:

THE HIGHER SELF

In life we are often seeking happiness outside of ourselves by buying materialistic items, smoking, drinking, or by attempting to get it from other people, but none of these things when obtained can satisfy us. Even Dorothy from the Wizard of Oz, tried to reveal to us that what we are always searching for, is already with us. What we are seeking is already seeking us. We can only receive that which we already have. Seek ye first, the kingdom of God and all things shall be added onto you (Matt 6:33). Everything that we ask for in prayer, has already been given to us by God. All we must do is drop the "K" and begin to "SEE" it right in front of our inner eye, instead of "SEEKING" it outside of us. We must turn inwards for the satisfaction that we are yearning for. The happiness, love, and joy that people have been looking for, has been inside them this entire time. There's an old story spoken by wisemen, that God was asking the angels, where could he hide man's Divinity? The angels told God to "Hide it in the mountains", and God replied "No, because they will climb the mountains and find it". So, the Angel suggested to "Hide it in the Ocean", and God replied, "No they will swim there". Then finally God said, "I will hide it inside his heart, because he will never think to look there". Yet, we wonder why we are never satisfied.

Well, I believe this occurs because we are looking for love a.k.a God, in all the wrong places. To seek God externally, is considered leaving God. God is not just in the sky, he resides inside our hearts through the power of the "Holy Spirit", also known as the "Intercessor, or Advocate". The Holy Spirit, which The Source sent to us in the name of Christ Yeshua, will teach us all things and will remind us of everything that the Christ said. The Spirit will prevent our hearts from being troubled and afraid. To commune with the Holy Spirit, we must first understand how it works through us. Simon said, "In all thy getting, get understanding". Consequently, knowledge, wisdom, and understanding can lead us to the truth, and the truth shall set us free.

Part of the truth is that the body can be viewed as the bridge used to close this gap between the soul and spirit. By the grace of God, we can meld and incorporate the Holy Spirit with our soul, to guide our minds and our brains with every daily decision. The spoken word has tremendous power. We are all equipped with an intricate and highly tuned inner guidance system, which we can regularly tap into using our inner knowing abilities also known as intuition to receive psychic information from our inner spiritual soul-self.

"For we are all electrical beings with intelligence." -Yogananda

It's highly plausible to assume that by spending nine months in our mother's dark womb, we became disconnected from the light within, referred to as the "Word of God and/or the Holy Spirit". This Spirit that once nourished us was replaced by another source or substitute. The substitute is the Egoic self, which is the surface part of our personalities that has been shaped by the world's programming or "Matrix". If we live too much in our ego self, we fall out of alignment with our spiritual self. Leading us to forgot about God's Divinity placed within us. Well now the new current energy of this Age of Aquarius is supporting us to re-member, meaning to rejoin with this Holy spiritual aspect of ourselves. Similar to the Bible story of the "Prodigal Son", when he came to his senses and remembered that his father's servants had food to spare, but he was starving to death, he soon returned home to the Father, who said, "Quick brings the best amenities for my son who was once spiritually dead and is alive again".

We are all a sliver of Source and if this sliver vanishes for a split second, we cease to exist as we know it. This sliver of Source can be compared to the entire ocean in one drop. That one drop carries magnificent power. Power beyond imagination. Once an individual begins to work with the power of the sliver and begin applying it to all walks of their life, reality can be transformed into whatever seed is being planted. We know that from an apple seed, is an apple, and from an acorn is an oak tree. If your seed is a desire for love, health, happiness, wealth, prosperity or success, then the sliver of power can help to grow that seed into your desired fruit. This magnificent power carries a magnetism strong enough to attract anything you want to be, do, or have.

Once a person begins to work with this sacred knowledge, they will no longer have to live in survival mode. Survival mode only happens when you don't know who you are, or whose you are. Neither do you know the person you want to become. The goal of survival mode is just to make it another day. However, God wants you to prosper. You will begin to feel like before starting this journey, you were on the outside looking in, now you are on the inside looking out. Putting a true meaning to being in the world, but not if it. Which is a very liberating thought and sense of being, leading to complete peace, and joy. Going from shades of nights to planes of light.

CHAPTER 10:

THE ULTIMATE GOAL: SELF-MASTERY

Self-mastery is like becoming the boss of your own life. It's about learning to control your thoughts, feelings, and actions so that you can be the best version of yourself. Just like a superhero learns to use their powers for good, self-mastery helps you use your strengths and talents to achieve your goals and dreams.

One important part of self-mastery is self-awareness. This means knowing yourself well—what makes you happy, what makes you sad, and what you're good at. It's like looking in a mirror and seeing yourself clearly, without any filters or distractions. When you're self-aware, you can make better decisions and understand why you feel certain ways.

Another part of self-mastery is self-discipline. This means being able to control your actions, even when you don't feel like it. It's like having a remote control for your behavior—you can choose to do things that help you reach your goals, even when it's hard. Self-discipline helps you stay focused and motivated, even when things get tough.

To master yourself, it's important to set goals for yourself and work towards them every day. This might mean practicing a skill you want to get better at, like playing an instrument or learning a new language. It could also mean being kind to others and treating them with respect, even when they're not being nice to you. By setting goals and working towards them, you can become the person you want to be and achieve great things in your life.

Self-mastery isn't something that happens overnight—it takes time and practice. But the more you work at it, the better you'll get. And the best part is, once you've mastered yourself, there's no limit to what you can achieve. You'll be able to face any challenge with confidence and courage, knowing that you have the power to overcome anything that comes your way. Keep working hard, stay focused on your goals, and never stop believing in yourself. With self-mastery, the sky's the limit!

CHAPTER 11:

THE POWER OF KNOWING YOUR SPIRIT GUIDES

Have you ever felt like there's someone watching over you, guiding you through life's ups and downs? That someone might be your spirit guide—a special friend from the spirit world who is always by your side, offering wisdom, support, and love. But how do you know who your spirit guides are, and how can you connect with them?

Imagine your spirit guides as wise and loving mentors who have been with you since the day you were born. They know you better than anyone else and are always there to help you navigate life's twists and turns. Some people have one main spirit guide, while others have a whole team of guides who work together to support them.

One way to connect with your spirit guides is through meditation and quiet reflection. Close your eyes, take a deep breath, and imagine yourself surrounded by a circle of light. Ask your spirit guides to reveal themselves to you, and pay attention to any thoughts, feelings, or images that come to mind. Your guides might communicate with you through your intuition, dreams, or subtle signs and synchronicities in your everyday life.

Once you've connected with your spirit guides, you can ask them for guidance and support whenever you need it. Whether you're facing a big decision, dealing with a challenging situation, or simply seeking comfort and reassurance, your guides are always there to lend a helping hand. Trust that they have your best interests at heart and are always working behind the scenes to help you fulfill your purpose and achieve your dreams.

Knowing your spirit guides is like having a secret superpower that gives you strength, courage, and confidence in everything you do. It's a reminder that you are never alone and that there is always someone watching over you, guiding you on your journey through life. Take the time to connect with your spirit guides, listen to their wisdom, and embrace the power of knowing that you are always supported and loved, no matter what challenges you may face.

CHAPTER 12:
THE INCREDIBLE POWER OF IMAGINATION

Imagine a world where anything is possible—a world where you can fly like a bird, explore distant galaxies, or build towering castles out of thin air. This world exists inside your imagination, a magical place where dreams come to life and possibilities are endless. But imagination is not just about escaping to far-off lands—it's also a powerful tool that can help us solve problems, express ourselves creatively, and achieve our goals.

One of the amazing things about imagination is that it allows us to see things in new and different ways. When we use our imagination, we can come up with creative solutions to problems that seemed impossible before. For example, imagine you have a big project due at school, but you're not sure how to start. By using your imagination, you might come up with a unique idea or approach that sets your project apart from the rest. Imagination helps us think outside the box and see things from a fresh perspective, which can lead to breakthroughs and discoveries.

Imagination is also a powerful tool for self-expression. Whether it's through art, music, writing, or storytelling, imagination allows us to share our thoughts, feelings, and ideas with others in a way that is uniquely our own. For example, a painter might use their imagination to create a beautiful masterpiece that evokes emotion and inspires awe in those who see it. Similarly, a writer might use their imagination to craft a compelling story that transports readers to another time and place. Imagination gives us the freedom to express ourselves in ways that are limitless and boundless.

But perhaps the most amazing thing about imagination is its ability to turn dreams into reality. When we imagine something, we create a vision of what we want our future to look like. This vision becomes a guiding light that inspires us to act and turn our dreams into reality. For example, imagine you dream of becoming a doctor and helping people in need. By using your imagination to visualize yourself achieving this goal, you can inspire yourself to work hard, overcome obstacles, and make your dream a reality. Imagination is like a roadmap that leads us towards our dreams, guiding us every step of the way.

In conclusion, imagination is a truly incredible power that lies within each one of us. It allows us to see the world in new and exciting ways, express ourselves creatively, and turn our dreams into reality. Whether we're solving problems, creating art, or pursuing our goals, imagination is the key that unlocks endless possibilities and propels us towards a brighter and more fulfilling future. So let your imagination soar and embrace the incredible power that lies within you!

'Imagination is more important than knowledge"-Albert Einstein

CHAPTER 13

THE GIFT OF PROSPERITY

God is the giver and the gift. In the Bible, there are many verses that talk about the gift of prosperity and how to gain it. But what does prosperity really mean? Prosperity isn't just about having a lot of money or possessions—it's about living a rich and fulfilling life, both in mind and spirit. It's about feeling happy, healthy, and grateful for all the blessings in our lives, big and small.

One verse that talks about prosperity is Jeremiah 29:11, which says, "For I know the plans I have for you, declares the Lord, plans to prosper you and not harm you, to give you a future and a hope." This verse reminds us that God has good plans for us and wants us to prosper in all areas of our lives. It's like a promise from God that if we trust in Him and follow His guidance, He will lead us to prosperity and abundance.

Another verse that talks about prosperity is Psalm 1:1-3, which says, "Blessed is the man who walks not in the counsel of the wicked, nor stands in the way of sinners, nor sits in the seat of scoffers; but his delight is in the law of the Lord, and on his law, he meditates day and night. He is like a tree planted by streams of water that yields its fruit in its season, and its leaf does not wither. In all that he does, he prospers." This verse reminds us that true prosperity comes from delighting in God's word and following His commandments. When we do this, it's like planting ourselves by a stream of water that nourishes us and helps us grow strong and fruitful.

So how do we gain prosperity according to the Bible? It's not just about material wealth, but about cultivating a mindset of abundance and gratitude. It's about trusting in God's plans for us and following His guidance in all that we do. It's about delighting in His word and living according to His commandments. When we do these things, we open ourselves up to the abundant blessings that God has in store for us, both in this life and in the life to come.

One way to gain prosperity is by setting goals and working hard to achieve them. This might mean studying hard in school, practicing a sport or hobby, or learning new skills that can help us succeed in the future. When we set goals and work towards them, it's like planting seeds of prosperity that can grow and flourish over time.

Another way to gain prosperity is by being grateful for what we have and focusing on the positive things in our lives. This might mean taking time each day to think about the things we're thankful for, like our family, friends, and the opportunities we have. When we focus on gratitude, it's like opening ourselves up to the abundance of blessings that surround us and attracting better things into our lives. Additionally, gaining prosperity means taking care of ourselves and our bodies. This might mean eating healthy foods, getting enough sleep, and exercising regularly.

When we take care of our bodies, it's like investing in our future health and happiness, and laying the foundation for a prosperous life. Moreover, gaining prosperity also involves being kind and generous towards others. This might mean volunteering in our community, helping a friend in need, or simply being kind to everyone we meet. When we give back to others, it's like spreading the wealth of prosperity and abundance, and creating a ripple effect of goodness that benefits us all.

In conclusion, gaining prosperity is about more than just having money—it's about living a rich and fulfilling life in all areas. By setting goals, practicing gratitude, taking care of ourselves, and being kind to others, we can open ourselves up to the abundant blessings that life has to offer, and create a prosperous future for ourselves and those around us.

CHAPTER 14:

MONEY: THE GETTING POWER OF SELF-AWARENESS

Money is like a magic wand that can make our dreams come true—it has the power to buy us things we need and want, like toys, clothes, and even a home. But did you know that money is also connected to something deeper inside us? It's called self-awareness, and it's like a superpower that helps us understand ourselves better and achieve our goals.

Imagine you're on a treasure hunt, searching for hidden treasures buried deep within yourself. That's what self-awareness is all about—it's like digging deep inside your mind and heart to discover what makes you tick. When you know yourself well, you can make better decisions about how to spend and save your money. You can figure out what you really want and need, instead of just buying things because everyone else has them.

But self-awareness isn't just about knowing what you want—it's also about knowing what you're good at. Imagine you're a superhero with special powers, like flying or super strength. Self-awareness helps you discover your own superpowers, whether it's being good at math, playing music, or making people laugh. When you know what you're good at, you can use your talents to earn money doing things you love.

Self-awareness also helps you understand your feelings and how they affect your money. For example, if you're feeling sad or stressed, you might be tempted to spend money to make yourself feel better. But self-awareness helps you recognize when you're feeling emotional and find healthier ways to cope, like talking to a friend or going for a walk. It's like having a built-in alarm system that helps you stay on track with your money goals.

So, how do you gain the getting power of self-awareness? It starts with paying attention to yourself and how you feel. Take time to think about what makes you happy, what makes you mad, and what makes you feel proud. Talk to your parents, teachers, or friends about your thoughts and feelings—they can help you understand yourself better. And most importantly, be kind to yourself and remember that self-awareness is like a journey—it takes time and practice, but the rewards are worth it. Therefore, keep exploring, keep learning, and keep growing. With self-awareness by your side, you'll have the getting power to achieve your wildest dreams!

CHAPTER 15:

ATTAINING WEALTH

Attaining wealth through a spiritual mindset is about more than just having money—it's about finding abundance and fulfillment in all areas of our lives. Imagine wealth as a treasure chest filled with not just gold and jewels, but also love, joy, and peace. When we approach life with a spiritual mindset, we open ourselves up to the limitless possibilities of the universe and trust that everything we need will come to us in the right time and in the right way. By focusing on gratitude, positivity, and abundance, we can attract wealth and prosperity into our lives and create a sense of richness that goes beyond material possessions.

One way to attain wealth through a spiritual mindset is by practicing the law of attraction. This law states that like attracts like, so when we focus on positive thoughts and intentions, we attract positive experiences and opportunities into our lives. By visualizing our goals and dreams as if they have already come true, we can manifest them into reality and create the life we desire. Additionally, by letting go of limiting beliefs and fears about money, we can open ourselves up to the flow of abundance and allow wealth to come to us naturally. With a spiritual mindset, we can tap into the infinite abundance of the universe and create a life of wealth, prosperity, and fulfillment.

As we reach the end of our journey through the power of self-care, self-love, self-awareness, and self-mastery, let us take a moment to reflect on the incredible lessons we have learned along the way. Throughout this book, we have explored how nurturing ourselves on a spiritual level can lead to greater wealth, health, prosperity, money, and love in our lives.

By prioritizing self-care, we have discovered the importance of nourishing our minds, bodies, and spirits. Through practices like meditation, mindfulness, and self-reflection, we have learned to cultivate inner peace, balance, and harmony. We have embraced the power of self-love, recognizing that true happiness comes from within and that we are worthy of love and acceptance just as we are.

Through the journey of self-awareness, we have gained a deeper understanding of ourselves and our true desires. By tuning into our intuition and listening to the whispers of our hearts, we have learned to trust ourselves and follow the path that leads to our highest good. And through the practice of self-mastery, we have empowered ourselves to take control of our lives and create the future we desire.

As we close this chapter, let us carry with us the wisdom and insights we have gained from this journey. May we continue to prioritize self-care, self-love, self-awareness, and self-mastery in our lives, knowing that they are the keys to unlocking greater happiness, health, success, love, wealth, prosperity and money. And may we always remember that by nurturing ourselves on a spiritual level, we can create lives that are rich, fulfilling, and abundant in every way.